TABLE OF CONTENTS

Neurodiverse SUPERpowers

Neurodiverse people behave, think, and learn differently from people with neurotypical brains. Neurodiverse people might be autistic, live with ADHD, dyslexia, PTSD, Tourette's, or other things. Neurodiverse people's differences include strengths. In a word, neurodiverse people are awesome.

What are your superpowers?
Write them below!

1. _____
2. _____
3. _____
4. _____
5. _____
6. _____
7. _____
8. _____
9. _____
10. _____

A few examples of neurodiverse superpowers:

Creativity
Focus
Paying attention to detail
Caring about others
Curiosity
Solving problems
Asking great questions
Good memory
Remembering details
Fast thinking
Lots of energy
Good with numbers
Good with pictures
Doing puzzles

You're SUPER!

Safety Matters

Name 5 things you can do to stay safe when you're on an adventure? Write them here!

1._____

2. _____

3. _____

4. _____

5. _____

Turn over to see possible answers

- Make sure you can see the human you're with
- Set a meeting place in case you cannot find your human
- Know your human's phone number - write it here: _____
- Wear a brightly colored shirt
- If you feel lost, ask a police officer or information human for help

Don't Leave Home Without It

What are 5 things you want to bring on your adventure with Rocket? Write them here!

1._____

2. _____

3. _____

4. _____

5. _____

Examples of things to bring on an adventure

- Water
- Healthy snacks
- Fidgets
- Tissues
- Devices to keep in touch
- Headphones
- Paper, pencil, crayons
- Card game
- Sweatshirt
- Money
- The phone number of the human you're adventuring with
- Rocket Around Washington DC Visual Guide and Activity Book!

Fun Facts about Washington DC Sites

Draw a line from the fact on the left to the correct site on the right

Facts

Sites

Years ago, the land at this site was a village where slaves going to freedom could get housing, education, and medical care.

National Museum of American History

You may have seen pictures of this site before – it appears on the back of the five-dollar bill. Ask your parents to show you.

Korean War Veterans Memorial

The statues in this site are constructed to make you feel that at least one is looking at you wherever you stand.

National World War II Memorial

There are 4,048 gold stars around this memorial! – one for every 100 American soldiers who lost their lives in the war.

The Lincoln Memorial

Washington Monument

When it was completed in 1884, this was the tallest building in the world (more than 555 feet tall)! Now there are lots of taller buildings. How many feet taller is it than you?

Arlington National Cemetery

6

Fun Facts about Washington DC Sites - ANSWERS

Facts

Sites

Years ago, the land at this site was a village where slaves going to freedom could get housing, education, and medical care.

You may have seen pictures of this site before – it appears on the back of the five-dollar bill. Ask your parents to show you.

The statues on this site are constructed to make you feel that at least one is looking at you wherever you stand.

There are 4,048 gold stars around this memorial! – one for every 100 American soldiers who lost their lives in the war.

When it was completed in 1884, this was the tallest building in the world (more than 555 feet tall)! Now there are lots of taller buildings. How many feet taller is it than you?

Korean War Veterans Memorial

National World War II Memorial

The Lincoln Memorial

Washington Monument

Arlington National Cemetery

GREAT Work!

Fun Facts continued

Facts

Sites

This museum calls its interactive experience for children STEAM (science, technology, engineering, arts, and math).

National Museum of the American Indian

This museum has 145 million live specimens and artifacts showing the history of Earth and helping humans understand the world and their place in it.

National Air and Space Museum

The panels on the exterior of this museum are designed to be just like a crown on the head of a statue inside the museum.

National Museum of African American History and Culture

More than 311 million people have visited this museum since it opened in 1976.

National Children's Museum

As of 2020, 9.2 million Americans describe themselves as having their ancestry honored through this museum.

National Museum of Natural History

Use those SUPERPowers!

Fun Facts continued - ANSWERS

Facts

This museum calls its interactive experience for children STEAM (science, technology, engineering, arts, and math).

This museum has 145 million live specimens and artifacts showing the history of Earth and helping humans understand the world and their place in it.

The panels on the exterior of this museum are designed to be just like a crown on the head of a statue inside the museum.

More than 311 million people have visited this museum since it opened in 1976.

As of 2020, 9.2 million Americans describe themselves as having their ancestry honored through this museum.

Sites

National Museum of the American Indian

National Air and Space Museum

National Museum of African American History and Culture

National Children's Museum

National Museum of Natural History

Word Search #1

Look left-to-right, up-to-down, and diagonal for the words below

1. Artifact
2. Washington
3. Owney
4. Memorial
5. Capitol
6. Botanic
7. Lincoln
8. Jefferson
9. Paddle
10. Tidal

```
S S G B O T A N I C R Y I C H S V S G J
S O Y G C O J J O I A T V A T H R U W O
H K M K S N M E X U F M V C E L I M L D
V I E E N N O F F L J R X E Q P U T W O
J Y T Q Y S N F A R A D G B P R E P A W
B P R Z P T U E L U R S G R A P M F S N
E P O B A D M R A N O R M J D K L B H E
L V M M R O E S O H I O H K D X V B I Y
Z M C F T G N O L C O C U O L C H T N W
N E X F I B T N X H J K S R E S N Y G V
S M G A F W U D Y A D E I E X D I F T X
P O W U A S X K A W G T Y A V S X D O G
K R K R C U U F E P X I J N T A M V N L
X I C T T H N Y K O K K A J W J I J A I
P A J Z B O X Q X S P I G C E J P P K B
N L D Z G B F O V T H M S C T I D A L R
A V M H U R C D J A K U O O H F W G R A
P A L I N C O L N L H G M S S V Q U G R
D O G S M Y C C C P V G E A Y P R G Z Y
F N Z C A P I T O L O X E G N W K C J L
```

Word Search #1 ANSWERS

Look left-to-right, up-to-down, and diagonal for the words below

1. ~~Artifact~~
2. ~~Washington~~
3. ~~Owney~~
4. ~~Memorial~~
5. ~~Capitol~~
6. ~~Botanic~~
7. ~~Lincoln~~
8. ~~Jefferson~~
9. ~~Paddle~~
10. ~~Tidal~~

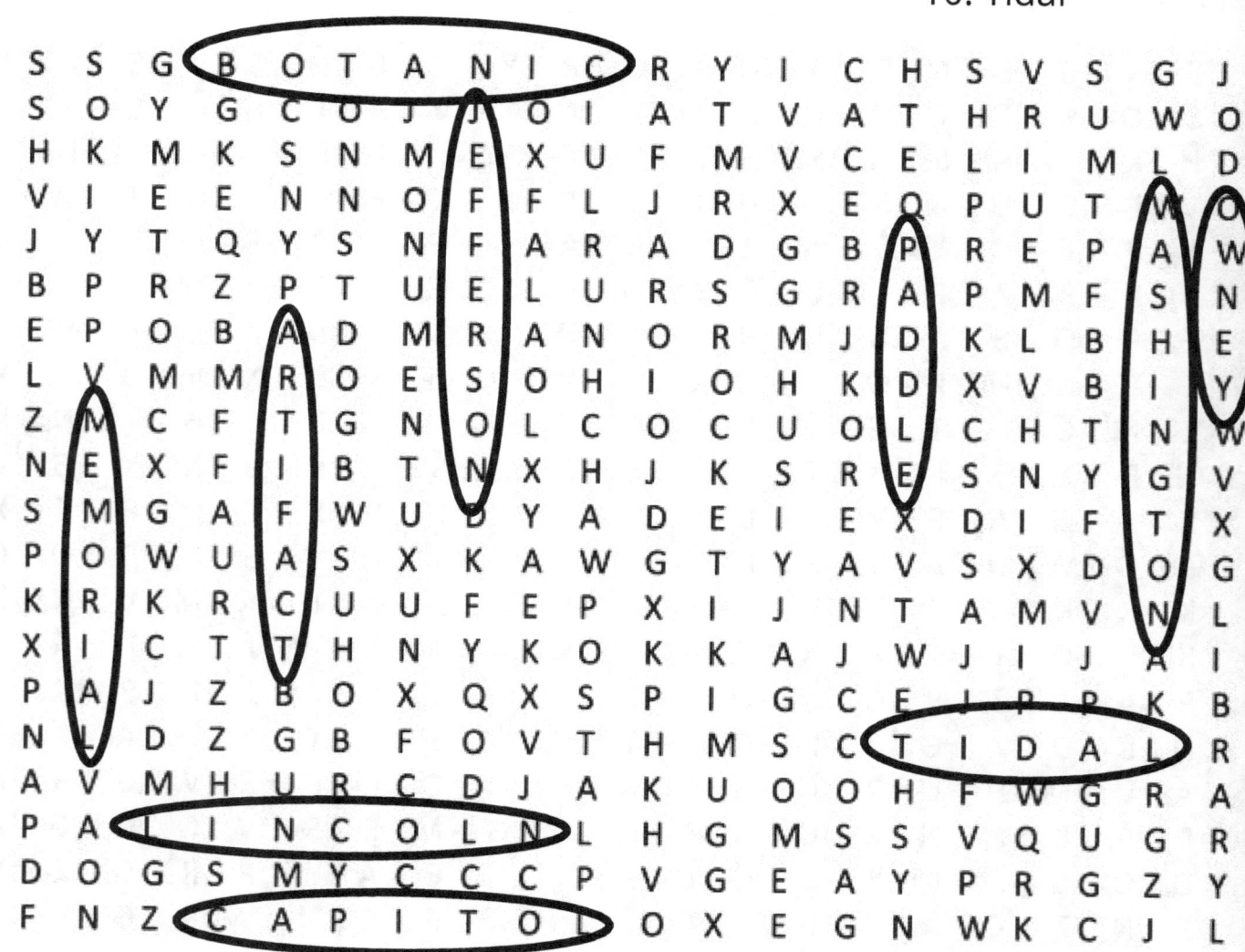

Word Search #2

Look left-to-right, up-to-down, and diagonal for the words below

1. Dogs
2. Rocket
3. Human
4. Nap
5. Monument
6. Korean
7. Library
8. Postal
9. Fala
10. Metro

```
S S G B O T A N I C R Y I C H S V S G J
S O Y G C O J J O I A T V A T H R U W O
H K M K S N M E X U F M V C E L I M L D
V I E E N N O F F L J R X E Q P U T W O
J Y T Q Y S N F A R A D G B P R E P A W
B P R Z P T U E L U R S G R A P M F S N
E P O B A D M R A N O R M J D K L B H E
L V M M R O E S O H I O H K D X V B I Y
Z M C F T G N O L C O C U O L C H T N W
N E X F I B T N X H J K S R E S N Y G V
S M G A F W U D Y A D E I E X D I F T X
P O W U A S X K A W G T Y A V S X D O G
K R K R C U U F E P X I J N T A M V N L
X I C T T H N Y K O K K A J W J I J A I
P A J Z B O X Q X S P I G C E J P P K B
N L D Z G B F O V T H M S C T I D A L R
A V M H U R C D J A K U O O H F W G R A
P A L I N C O L N L H G M S S V Q U G R
D O G S M Y C C C P V G E A Y P R G Z Y
F N Z C A P I T O L O X E G N W K C J L
```

12

Word Search #2 ANSWERS

Look left-to-right, up-to-down, and diagonal for the words below

1. ~~Dogs~~
2. ~~Rocket~~
3. ~~Human~~

4. ~~Nap~~
5. ~~Monument~~
6. ~~Korean~~

7. ~~Library~~
8. ~~Postal~~
9. ~~Fala~~
10. ~~Metro~~

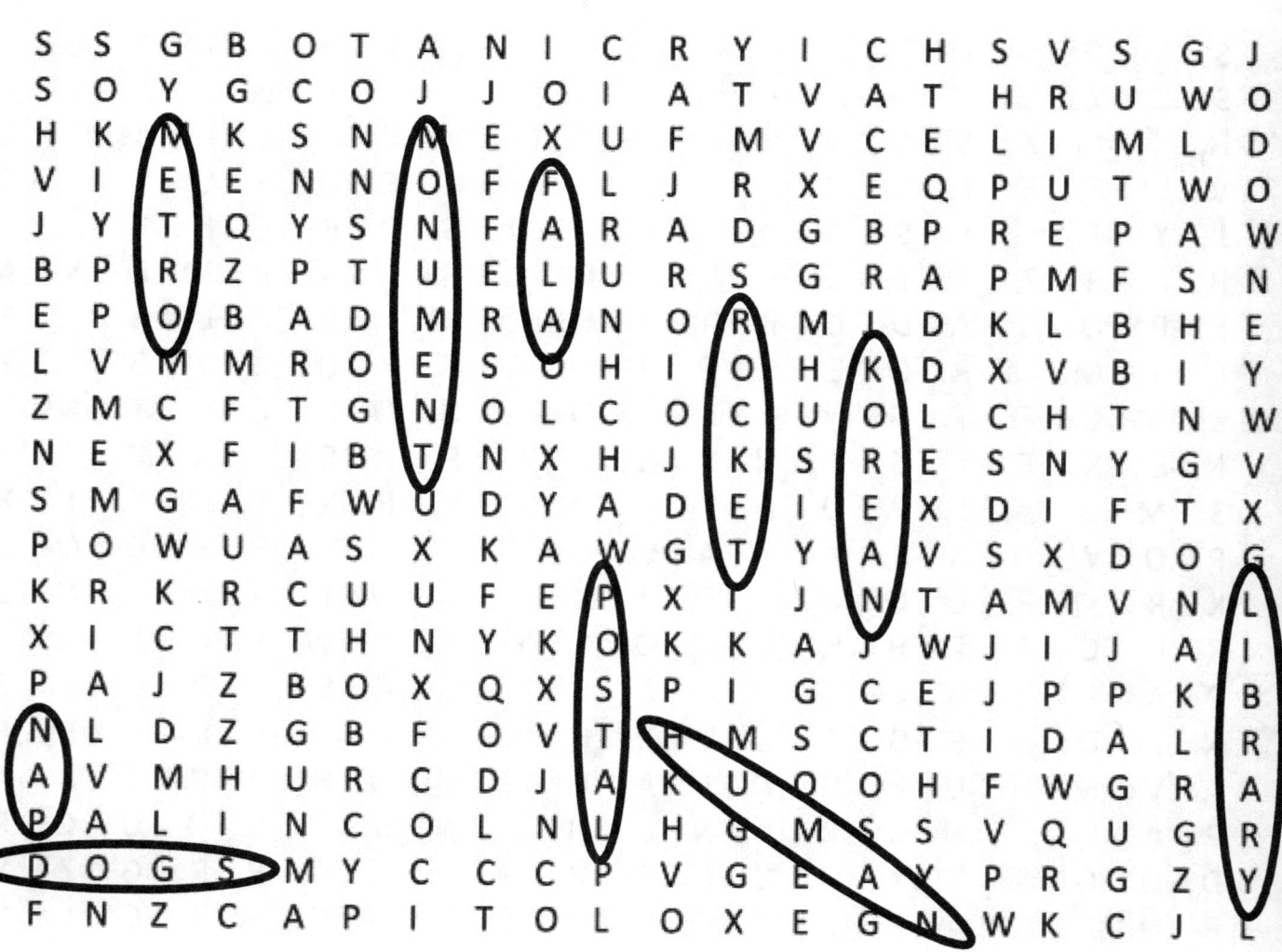

Rocket at The White House Coloring Page

Pattern Play

Look at the position of each of the DC sites in the chart below. Which sites would continue the pattern? See the answers on the next page.

Pattern Play ANSWERS

Look at the position of each of the DC sites in the chart below. Which sites would continue the pattern? See the answers on the next page.

DC Memorials and Monuments

Write the name of each memorial or monument next to each picture

Write the names below next to pictures at left (see answers on the next page):

Lincoln Memorial

MLK Jr. Memorial

FDR Memorial

Korean War Memorial

Jefferson Memorial

Washington Monument

DC Memorials and Monuments ANSWERS

Write the name of each memorial or monument next to each picture

Jefferson Memorial

MLK Jr. Memorial

Write the names below next to pictures at left (see answers on the next page):

Lincoln Memorial

MLK Jr. Memorial

FDR Memorial

Korean War Memorial

Jefferson Memorial

Washington Monument

FDR Memorial

Lincoln Memorial

Korean War Memorial

Washington Monument

DC Museums

Write the name of each memorial or monument next to each picture

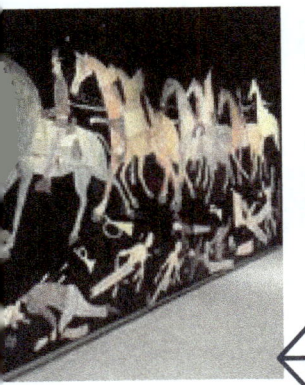

Write the names below next to pictures at left (see answers on the next page):

National Museum of African American History and Culture

Museum of the American Indian

National Air and Space Museum

National Museum of Natural History

National Children's Museum

DC Museums ANSWERS

Write the name of each memorial or monument next to each picture

National Air and Space Museum

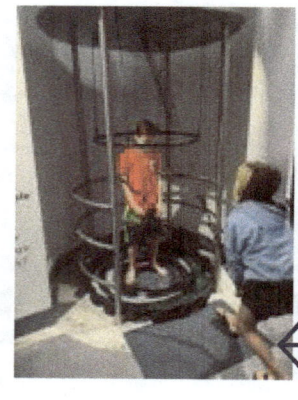

National Children's Museum

Write the names below next to pictures at left (see answers on the next page,

National Museum of African American History and Culture

Museum of the American Indian

National Museum of African American History and Culture

Museum of the American Indian

National Air and Space Museum

National Museum of Natural History

National Museum of Natural History

National Children's Museum

Ready, Set, Guess!

The Smithsonian Institution includes 19 museums, 21 libraries, nine research centers, and a zoo. Most are located in Washington DC, and many are free to enter. Write the name of each Smithsonian building next to the pictures on the left.

Write the names below next to pictures at left (see answers on the next page):

National Museum of African American History and Culture

National Air and Space Museum

National Museum of Natural History

National Museum of American History

National Postal Museum

Smithsonian Institution

Ready, Set, Guess! ANSWERS

The Smithsonian Institution includes 19 museums, 21 libraries, nine research centers, and a zoo. Most are located in Washington DC, and many are free to enter. Write the name of each Smithsonian building next to the pictures on the left.

National Museum of American History

Museum of African American History

National Museum of Natural History

Smithsonian Institution

National Air and Space Museum

National Postal Museum

Write the names below next to pictures at left (see answers on the next page)

National Museum of African American History and Culture

National Air and Space Museum

National Museum of Natural History

National Museum of American History

National Postal Museum

Smithsonian Institution

DC By the Numbers

See the answers on the next page

Which of the numbers on the right match these facts? Write them below

Gravesites for veterans at Arlington National Cemetery _____

People who visit the Lincoln Memorial each year _____

Columns at the National World War II Memorial _____

Feet in height of the Washington Monument _____

Additional books and other items added to the Library of Congress every day _____

Cherry blossom trees bloom around the Jefferson Memorial and Tidal Basin each Spring _____

14,000+

7 million

56

600

10,000

3,700

26

DC By the Numbers ANSWERS

Gravesites for veterans at Arlington National Cemetery - 14,000+

People who visit the Lincoln Memorial each year - 7 million

Columns at the National World War II Memorial - 56

Feet in height of the Washington Monument - 600

Additional books and other items added to the Library of Congress every day - 10,000

Cherry blossom trees bloom around the Jefferson Memorial and Tidal Basin each Spring - 3,700

You're SUPER!

14,000+

7 million

56

600

10,000

3,700

Rocket versus DC Friends

Rocket loves to play wrestle.
Who would you choose in these epic showdowns?

Rocket versus the ducks in the U.S. Capitol reflecting pool

Why Rocket?
Fast
Wrestles alot
Bigger

Why the ducks?
Can fly
Loud
Kind of slippery

Rocket says: He could wrestle a whole flock of ducks!

Rocket versus mega whale at Museum Natural History

Why Rocket?
Fast
Fierce bark
Sneaky

Why the shark?
Big
Really big
Scary looking

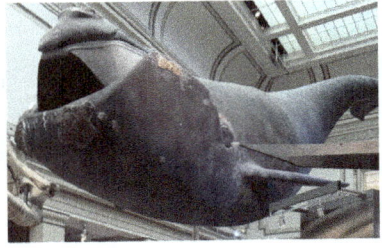

Rocket says: He's rather not talk about who might come out on top

Rocket versus Owney the mail dog at the Postal Museum

Why Rocket?
Fast
Not stuffed
Small and scrappy

Why Owney?
Bigger
In better shape
Stronger

Rocket says: They would tie - and be best friends!

28

The National Mall & Downtown Washington DC

Match the numbers to the sites on the next page. Color the map!

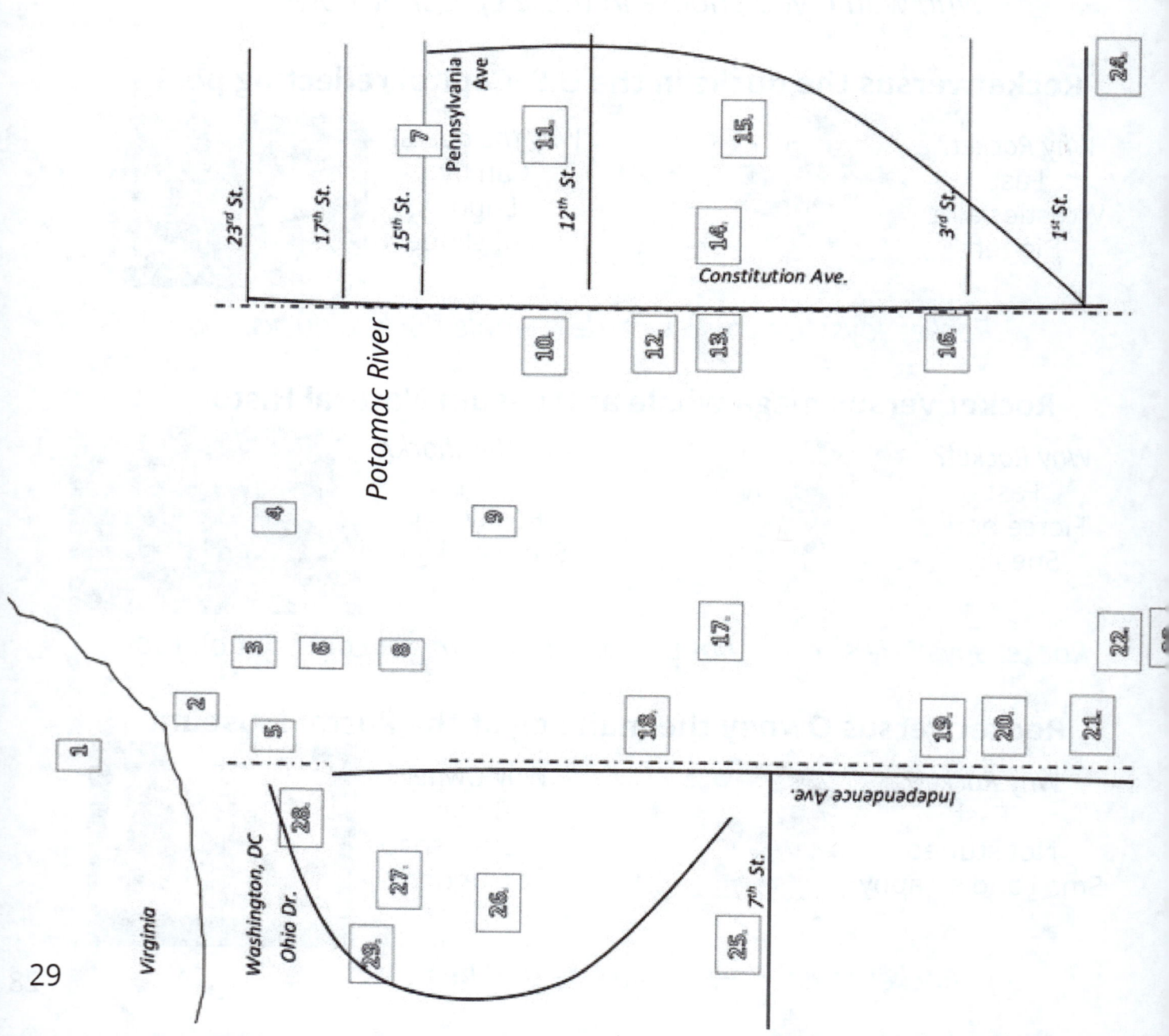

29

What's on The DC Map

1. Arlington National Cemetery
2. Memorial Bridge
3. Lincoln Memorial
4. Vietnam Memorial
5. Korean War Veterans Memorial
6. National World War II Memorial
7. The White House
8. Washington Monument
9. National Museum of African American History and Culture
10. National Museum of American History
11. National Children's Museum
12. National Museum of Natural History
13. National Gallery of Art Sculpture Garden
14. National Archives Building
15. National Portrait Gallery
16. National Gallery of Art
17. Carousel on the Mall
18. Smithsonian 'castle' (Smithsonian Institution Building)
19. National Air and Space Museum
20. National Museum of the American Indian
21. U.S. Botanic Garden
22. United States Capitol
23. Library of Congress
24. National Postal Museum
25. International Spy Museum
26. Jefferson Memorial
27. Tidal Basin
28. MLK (Martin Luther King) Memorial
29. FDR (Franklin Delano Roosevelt) Memorial

- - - - - - - - - - - - -
The National Mall - - - - - - - - - - - -

Note: Most streets do not appear on the map.

What in the WORD?!

Write words in the blanks below. Read the story to your favorite human.

Today my _____ family is going to the District of
Columbia, also known as _____ or just
_____. It's the capital of the
_____.
I _____ seeing new places. DC is not far from my
house. I just know they are taking me with them! They wouldn't leave
_____ behind, right?
They're zipping up their _____ so we must be
leaving.
And they are out the _____!
Wait – what about _____? They must not know
they left me _____.
I'll try the back _____...Hi-ya! I am
_____!!
Now, where did they go? Sniff, sniff - I smell
_____! Come with me!
They hopped on the _____to go into the city. We
will too.
We're probably not supposed to be on here alone, so we'll just
_____under this _____.

COMIC STRIP

Rocket's perfect job -- working at the U.S. Postal Museum

Scavenger Hunt

Find the pictures of the things below on the pages of this book (look on all pages) or find them in Washington DC. See answers on the next page.

1. Carousel on the National Mall
2. Stamp of Owney the U.S. Postal Service dog at the National Postal Museum
3. Ducks in the Capitol Hill reflecting pool
4. Fala at the FDR Memorial
5. Giant spider at the National Gallery of Art Sculpture Garden
6. Giant shark hanging on the ceiling of the National Museum of Natural History
7. Horses in the painting of Battle of Little Big Horn, National Museum of the American Indian
8. Man and dog crossing country in an old-time car, National Museum of American History
9. Sydney, the first dog to go to Antarctica, National Air and Space Museum
10. The words of Abraham Lincoln's Gettysburg Address
11. Soldiers at the Korean War Memorial
12. Yawning Tiger, National Gallery of Art (by Anna Hyatt Huntington)

You can do it!

Scavenger Hunt - ANSWERS

1. Carousel on the National Mall, page 35
2. Stamp of Owney the U.S. Postal Service dog at the National Postal Museum, pages 28, 38 and 40
3. Ducks in the Capitol Hill reflecting pool, pages 28, 38 and 40
4. Fala at the FDR Memorial, page 20, 21, 38 and 40
5. Giant spider at the National Gallery of Art Sculpture Garden, pages 18, 29, and 35
6. Giant whale hanging on the ceiling of the National Museum of Natural History, pages 24, 25, 28, 38 and 40
7. Horses in the painting of Battle of Little Big Horn, National Museum of the American Indian, pages 23 and 24
8. Man and dog crossing country in an old-time car, National Museum of American History, pages 24 and 25
9. Sydney, the first dog to go to Antarctica, National Air and Space Museum, page 35
10. The words of Abraham Lincoln's Gettysburg Address, pages 18 and 19
11. Soldiers at the Korean War Memorial, pages 20 and 21
12. Yawning Tiger, National Gallery of Art (by Anna Hyatt Huntington), page 35

Rocket Around DC Game Board
See directions on the next page and HAVE FUN!

FINISH!

START

Rocket Around DC Board Game Directions

The goal of the game is to get from the START to the FINISH first using your board game piece. Here's how to play:

1. Cut out the board game character and number pieces on the next page.
2. Each player chooses a board game character piece.
3. Fold each character piece at the word FOLD and put each piece at the START square on the board game.
4. Cut out the board game number pieces on the next page. Put each number face down in the middle of the board game.
5. Each player picks a number - the person with the highest number goes first. If a player gets a Back 1 or Skip turn piece, draw again.
6. Put the numbers face down again in the middle of the board. Keep choosing numbers until each player's position to start is determined.
7. To start, put the numbers face down again in the middle of the board. The first player will choose a number, move that many spaces on the board, put their number face down again in the middle of the board, and shuffle the numbers around.
8. When it's a new player's turn, they will choose a number, move that many spaces on the board, put their number face down again in the middle of the board, and shuffle the numbers around.
9. Continue to move in the same order by picking a game number piece until someone reaches the FINISH square and WINS!
10. When you're done, put the game pieces in the back pocket of this book.

HAVE FUN!

Board Game Pieces

Cut out the board game pieces below to play the Rocket Around DC Board Game

Board Game Character Pieces

Capitol reflecting pool duck (FOLD)

Mega whale Natural History (FOLD)

Owney - Postal Museum (FOLD)

African elephant Natural History (FOLD)

Fala - FDR's pup (FOLD)

Board Game Number Pieces

1	1	1	1	Back 1	Skip turn
2	2	2	3	3	4

Extra Board Game Pieces

Use these in case any pieces get lost

Board Game Character Pieces

Capitol reflecting pool duck (FOLD)

Mega whale Natural History (FOLD)

Owney - Postal Museum (FOLD)

African elephant Natural History (FOLD)

Fala - FDR's pup (FOLD)

Board Game Number Pieces

1	1	1	1	Back 1	Skip turn

2	2	2	3	3	4

Storage Pocket for Board Game Pieces

How to use this page:

- *Cut it out along the dotted line.*
- *Tape or staple sides 1, 2, and 3 of this page on the inside of the back cover of this book.*
- *Do not tape or staple side 4 - it needs to remain open.*
- *Slide the board pieces from the previous page into the open side 4 and store your board game pieces there when you are not using them.*

SIDE 3

Tape or staple this side on back cover

Tape or staple this side on back cover

SIDE 1

Tape or staple this side on back cover

SIDE 2

Be a Rocketarounder!

1. Share Rocket's values of building your brain through adventure, imagination, and finding new ways to have fun!

2. Do all of the activities in the *Rocket Around Washington DC - Neurodiverse activity + coloring book for kids.* Which Rocket Around books have you read? Write them here: _____

_____

3. Where should Rocket and his humans go next? Where would your dog want to rocket around with Rocket? Email your ideas to Rocket at lee@rocketaround.com (make sure your mom or dad is okay with it first).

<u>Congratulations, you are an official Rocketarounder - welcome to the Club!</u>

<u>I'M A ROCKETAROUNDER!</u>
I build my brain through:
-*Adventure*
-*Imagination*
-*Finding new ways to have fun!*

44

ISBN: 979-8-9889331-3-7
Text copyright 2023.
Illustrations copyright 2023.
All rights reserved. Published by Rocket Around LLC.
Printed in the U.S.A.

Rocket Around books:
Rocket Around Washington DC - A Neurodiverse Visual Guide for Kids
Rocket Around Washington DC eBook
Rocket Around Washington DC - A Neurodiverse Activities + Coloring Book

Look for these books and other fun kids' activities at rocketaround.com